BAR MITZVAH BOY

BAR MITZVAH BOY

BY MARK LEIREN-YOUNG

PLAYWRIGHTS CANADA PRESS
TORONTO

For professional or amateur production rights, please contact:
Michael Petrasek at Kensington Literary Representation
34 St. Andrew Street, Toronto, ON M5T 1K6
416.848.9648 :: kensingtonlit@rogers.com

LIBRARY AND ARCHIVES CANADA CATALOGUING IN PUBLICATION
Title: Bar mitzvah boy / Mark Leiren-Young.
Names: Leiren-Young, Mark, author.
Description: First edition. | A play.
Identifiers: Canadiana (print) 20200172506 | Canadiana (ebook) 20200172514 | ISBN 9780369100689 (softcover) | ISBN 9780369100696 (PDF) | ISBN 9780369100702 (EPUB) | ISBN 9780369100719 (Kindle)
Classification: LCC PS8573.E478 B37 2020 | DDC C812/.54—dc23

Playwrights Canada Press acknowledges that we operate on land, which, for thousands of years, has been the traditional territories of the Mississaugas of the Credit, Wendat, Anishinaabe, Métis, and Haudenosaunee peoples. Today, this meeting place is home to many Indigenous peoples from across Turtle Island and we are grateful to have the opportunity to work and play here.

We acknowledge the financial support of the Canada Council for the Arts—which last year invested $153 million to bring the arts to Canadians throughout the country—the Ontario Arts Council (OAC), Ontario Creates, and the Government of Canada for our publishing activities.

Canada Council for the Arts | Conseil des arts du Canada

ONTARIO ARTS COUNCIL
CONSEIL DES ARTS DE L'ONTARIO
an Ontario government agency
un organisme du gouvernement de l'Ontario

Canada

ONTARIO CREATES | ONTARIO CRÉATIF

For my mom, Carol Leiren. I guess it was worth sending me to Talmud Torah.

KOSHER THEATRE

Bar Mitzvah Boy premiered at a Christian theatre.

The mandate for Pacific Theatre in Vancouver is, officially, to produce "faith-based" and "spiritual" theatre, but as pretty much any non-Christian will tell you, that's usually code for Christian . . . like "non-denominational" services that inevitably mention Jesus. And the theatre is located in an Anglican church. So even if Pacific isn't officially Christian, it's in a building with a lot more crosses than your average synagogue, mosque or Buddhist retreat.

When I sent them the script I wasn't interested in their religious leanings—I was excited about their track record of doing first-rate productions with Vancouver's best actors. So when Artistic Director Ron Reed said he wanted to premiere the play, I was happy to thank any deity willing to listen.

Then Ron asked if I had anyone in mind for the roles, and I gave him my initial suggestions for my rabbi and bar mitzvah boy. "I didn't realize they were Jewish," he said.

"They're not," I said, "but they're amazing."

They also weren't the amazing actors who did the show.

Richard Newman is, what we call, a member of the tribe. Gina Chiarelli—the original Rabbi Michael—not so much.

Richard knew all the prayers in the play. Gina was determined to conquer them. She wanted to learn how to say everything "correctly." The director, Ian Farthing, hired a Judaism consultant to help with prayers and rituals. Our consultant couldn't help with Gina's Hebrew because he was from Toronto and had an eastern accent that sounded off to a Vancouverite like me. Richard's originally from Chicago, so his accent sounded even stranger. Ian is Jewish, but still has an accent from England. I was useless because my Hebrew still has the Russian accent I learned from my grandfather.

I tracked down my friend Sandee Huberman, who I'd known since Talmud Torah elementary school. She'd recently moved to Israel and taped all the Hebrew for us. Gina mimicked Sandee's pronunciations and, when the play opened and audiences heard that one of the actors wasn't Jewish, some Jews in the crowd were convinced Richard was faking it.

Gina sounded local. Richard sounded wrong.

My cousin Zach, who was bar mitzvahed just before the play opened, said he thought Richard did a good job with the Hebrew, but he wasn't fooled for a minute.

I've told variations on this story in every talkback as someone in the audience—usually a Jewish someone—wants to confirm whether the actors (and I) are Jewish.

David Winitsky, artistic director of the Jewish Plays Project, who staged the debut reading in New York and has since been involved with readings in several other major US cities, jokes, "Any time you do something Jewish on stage—speak Hebrew or Yiddish, pray, cook—it is guaranteed that someone will tell you you're doing it wrong. They are both correct."

In a recent talkback, I mentioned that in my play *Shylock*, when an actor is told he can't play Othello, he replies, "Does that mean that every actor who plays Shylock has to be circumcised? I've heard of actors doing a lot of things for a role but . . . "

I wrote that over twenty years ago and—while I've never asked—I'd bet that not every actor who has done my *Shylock* would pass that test.

The other inevitable question is whether non-Jewish audiences "get" the play. I tell them the play's Canadian premiere was at a Christian theatre and the US debut was at a "secular" theatre.

I also mention that a couple of my favourite plays feature nuns. John Patrick Shanley's *Doubt* and Christopher Durang's *Sister Mary Ignatius Explains It All for You*. I'm pretty sure those aren't just for Catholics—although I suspect there are moments in each where Catholics wince or laugh a bit more than anyone else in the audience.

Most non-Jewish audience members won't know the lyrics to Adon Olam any better than I know the Catholic liturgy, but I suspect most of you know—or are—a Joey or a Michael searching for meaning or faith or some combination of the two.

—Mark Leiren-Young, April 2020

NOTES

Staging: The sets should be arranged to allow for smooth transitions with characters flowing between scenes. No blackouts should be required—other than the one after Scene Fourteen.

Final scene: If there are a lot of Jewish audience members they may want to sing along to Adon Olam. If you feel it will work for your audience, feel free to complete the prayer/song. Some producers have included transliterations of the prayer in their program so everyone can sing along.

Age: Please adjust the line on page 10, "Fifty-two years . . . Give or take," to fit the age of the actor instead of casting to fit the line. That is to say, if you find a Joey who reads as seventy-five, it should be: "Sixty-two years . . . Give or take."

Ball caps: Whatever team is chosen for Michael's ball cap, that team's sport is the one to reference when referring to G-d getting involved with sports. So if the cap is for a baseball team, reference baseball. If hockey, then switch to hockey. If soccer, thank you for staging this in Europe ☺.

G-d: When I was in Hebrew school I was taught that you never write the full name of G-d. Leonard Cohen uses "G-d," so I guess it's kosher. Unless noted it is pronounced as "God."

Pronunciations: Hebrew pronunciations shift between communities and regions. Please use the pronunciations most familiar to your region.

Tefillin: If you're right-handed, tefillin are always on the left arm, but lefties do their right arm. Michael's line on page 31 should be adjusted to suit the actor. Beyond that, different communities have different traditions here. You can consult a local expert or refer to a tefillin video online, such as https://www.youtube.com/watch?v=FjYB-ntmx-M&t=85s or https://www.myjewishlearning.com/article/tefillin-phylacteries/.

The shul: Schara Tzedeck is the orthodox synagogue in this world. If you'd like to use the name of your local orthodox synagogue, feel free. If there is a local Schara Tzedeck and you are concerned about using the name, feel free to use another name.

Prayers: Adon Olam "old version" = Gerovitch. New version = whichever non-Gerovitch version is used locally.

Other resources: There are multiple sources online offering help with transliteration and pronunciation. Here are a few that directors of *Bar Mitzvah Boy* have found helpful:

https://www.myjewishlearning.com

https://www.jewishvirtuallibrary.org

https://torahlessons.org

Bar Mitzvah Boy was first produced by Pacific Theatre in Vancouver, BC, in March 2018 with the following cast and creative team:

Rabbi Michael: Gina Chiarelli
Joey: Richard Newman
Voice of Sheryl: Jalen Saip

Director: Ian Farthing
Set Designer: Carolyn Rapanos
Lighting Designer: Jillian White
Sound Designer: Matthew MacDonald-Bain
Costume Designer: Kaitlin Williams
Props Master: Paige Louter
Stage Manager: April Starr Land
Technical Director: Kougar Basi
Dialogue Coach: Howard Siegel

The play was first produced in the United States by Chester Theatre Company in Chester, MA, in June 2018 with the following cast and creative team:

Rabbi Michael: Tara Franklin
Joey: Will LeBow

Director: Guy Ben-Aharon
Scenic Design: David Towlun
Costume Design: Charles Schoonmaker
Lighting Design: Lara Dubin
Sound Design: David Reiffel
Stage Manager: Laura Kathryne Gomez

The play won the 2017 Jewish Playwriting Contest from the Jewish Plays Project with a reading that featured Annie Meisels as Michael and Philip Hoffman as Joey, and was directed by David Winitsky, with sound design/composition by Mark Van Hare, lighting design by Joshua Benghiat, assistant direction and stage management by Lauren Shields, casting directed by Judy Bowman and dramaturgy by Jeremy Stoller.

The play has since gone on to have productions at the Harold Green Jewish Theatre Company in Toronto and at the West Coast Jewish Theatre in Los Angeles, and the Winnipeg Jewish Theatre.

THE CAST

Rabbi Michael Levitz-Sharon: mid-thirties to mid-forties.

Joey "Yosef" Brant: mid-sixties or better.

Sheryl: Never seen. She has the accent you want the woman who runs your local kosher deli to at least pretend to have.

THE TIME

This year. Our story begins in the summer. Ends in the fall.

THE SET

Jogging path.

Rabbi's office: Judaica, bookshelves, desk (no family photos).

The Bimah: the podium the rabbi delivers the service from. Ideally the set suggests (or shows) the ark in the background. There is an "eternal light" (ner tamid), which should be on before the audience enters and remain on until after the audience exits.

Joey's office: A high-end lawyer's office.

SCENE ONE

JOGGING PATH

Friday afternoon.

MICHAEL *jogs on stage carrying the weight of the world. She is dressed in sweats and a ball cap for a local sports team.*

MICHAEL *stops, continues running in place to check her pulse with two fingers to her neck, then keeps running off stage.*

SCENE TWO

RABBI'S OFFICE

Late Friday afternoon.

JOEY*'s back is towards us. He's decked out in prayer regalia—including tefillin, which are on incorrectly. He's checking the books and pulls one down, stops, pulls another, stops. He takes a hefty book and turns to face the audience, looking very much like the perfect rabbi.*

An old-style intercom buzzes and we hear the voice of SHERYL.

SHERYL: Rabbi. You've got a visitor. I said to wait in the hall but . . . Rabbi?

JOEY settles behind the desk. Relaxed. At home. He opens the book, flips the pages. MICHAEL enters, sweaty from her run. And . . .

MICHAEL: Excuse me.

JOEY: Hello.

MICHAEL stares at JOEY, puzzled.

What can I do for you? I'm sorry, I don't mean to be rude, but I'm waiting for someone.

MICHAEL: I see.

JOEY: I have an appointment.

MICHAEL: Sorry to disturb you.

JOEY: Not a problem, I'm sure the receptionist can help you out.

MICHAEL: Or security.

JOEY: Absolutely.

MICHAEL reaches for the intercom.

MICHAEL: Shall I call security?

JOEY: I'm sorry, do you work here? I don't know everyone who works here.

MICHAEL: I can see that.

JOEY extends a hand.

JOEY: Joey.

MICHAEL shakes.

MICHAEL: Michael.

JOEY: So your parents wanted a boy?

MICHAEL: It means "gift from G-d" or "who is like G-d."

JOEY: It means your parents wanted a boy.

MICHAEL: I'm guessing yours did too.

JOEY: So what do you do here?

MICHAEL: This and that . . . I'm the rabbi. So more this than that.

JOEY: No.

MICHAEL: And you're in my chair.

JOEY: You're Rabbi Levitz-Sharon? (*pronounced Share-in.*)

MICHAEL: Rabbi Michael Levitz-Sharon. (*pronounced Sha-rown*) Like the prime minister. No relation.

JOEY: But you're—

MICHAEL: Not circumcised?

JOEY: Young. I was thinking young.

MICHAEL: Of course you were.

JOEY indicates her ball cap.

JOEY: And that's your kippah? So you cover your head all the time?

MICHAEL: You must be Mr. Brant.

JOEY: So you heard I was coming?

MICHAEL: I heard you wanted to see me today and Sheryl told you I wasn't available because I'm never available Friday afternoons. I've got a service to prepare.

JOEY: Did she tell you it was an emergency? I told her to tell you it was an emergency.

MICHAEL: Did somebody die?

JOEY: No one I know.

MICHAEL: Is someone dying?

JOEY: We're all dying. It's the human condition.

MICHAEL: So it's not an emergency. And it's almost Shabbat. And I really have to shower and change.

JOEY: This won't take long.

MICHAEL: I can see you next week. Not on Friday. Once the sun goes down I can't turn on the hot water.

JOEY: That's just silly.

MICHAEL: It is, actually, but that's religion for you.

JOEY: An ancient tradition dating back to the great showers of Egypt.

MICHAEL: Also, the congregation will be wondering where I am.

JOEY: I'm here now. I'm dressed. I only need a minute.

MICHAEL: You look lovely. You should stay for services.

JOEY: Are you kidding? It's Friday night.

MICHAEL: Yes, that would be when we traditionally have Friday night services. And you know what happens at sundown?

JOEY: Hell yah. I remember this from Hebrew school. The chariot turns into a pumpkin and the horses turn back into mice.

MICHAEL: You have to go. I have to change. Now if you want to talk next week—

JOEY: This'll only take a second. Please, just one second, I promise.

MICHAEL considers, surrenders.

MICHAEL: Nu?

JOEY: So you'll listen?

MICHAEL: Will you leave if I don't?

JOEY: You know my grandson, Benny? Bright boy, sweet kid, the best. You know he's twelve and he's in your Hebrew school here and—

MICHAEL: One second.

JOEY: He's getting bar mitzvahed in November. He's getting bar mitzvahed here.

MICHAEL: Mazel tov.

JOEY: You don't know Benny?

MICHAEL: Cantor Reuben teaches the kids. I don't meet most of them till they start coming to shul to prepare for the big day. Benny Brant.

JOEY: Goldman. Ben Goldman.

MICHAEL: You're Tzeporah's dad?

JOEY: You know Sandee?

MICHAEL: From high school. I haven't seen her in years.

JOEY: Good, perfect, that's perfect.

MICHAEL: Ben's getting bar mitzvahed here? Not at the Schara Tzedeck?

JOEY: That's what it says on the invitations.

MICHAEL: You're Tzeporah's dad?

JOEY: She got her mother's looks.

MICHAEL: So Ben's getting bar mitzvahed in November. I suppose we'll see you then. Mazel tov. I've really got to—

JOEY: That's the thing. There's something I need to do before Benny's bar mitzvah.

MICHAEL, sympathetic, clues in.

MICHAEL: It's okay, Mr. Brant, a lot of people forget their Hebrew. If you're doing an aliyah you don't need to worry.

We have a sheet with all the Hebrew in transliteration . . . phonetic English . . . Not every Jew knows Hebrew anymore.

Just come to a few services before and you'll be fine. You don't strike me as the shy type.

JOEY: Transliteration. I like that. Is everything transliterated now?

MICHAEL: I really do need to change.

She takes her hoodie off, keeps her ball cap on, and starts gathering her clothes to change.

JOEY: It's not Benny's bar mitzvah I'm worried about . . . It's mine.

MICHAEL: What about yours?

JOEY: I need one . . . And it needs to happen before Benny's. Maybe next week. I'm clear Tuesday.

MICHAEL: Tuesday?

JOEY: Tuesday would be good—but I'm flexible. What day works for you?

MICHAEL: That's not how we do it.

JOEY: I'm dressed for it now.

MICHAEL: I'm not. You should stay for services.

JOEY: But it's Friday night.

MICHAEL: In less than an hour.

JOEY: Poker night.

MICHAEL: And that's your regular poker outfit?

JOEY *indicates the tallis.*

JOEY: Good place to hide an ace.

MICHAEL: You need to fix the tefillin.

JOEY: Wrong arm?

MICHAEL: That too.

JOEY: See, if I had a bar mitzvah I'd know that.

MICHAEL: This isn't Hogwarts. It's not like there's a magic spell and you suddenly learn everything you need to know. That's why there are classes. Months of classes.

JOEY: I'll make a donation.

MICHAEL: That would be lovely.

JOEY: And then you'll bar mitzvah me.

He takes out his wallet.

MICHAEL: No money on Shabbat.

JOEY: It's not sundown yet.

MICHAEL: Close enough.

JOEY: So I'll write you a cheque.

MICHAEL: Still Shabbat.

JOEY: When are we doing this?

MICHAEL: After you go to class. Tuesdays and Thursdays. Four thirty. Cantor Reuben.

JOEY: You want me in Benny's class?

MICHAEL: It's the only class we've got. Cantor Reuben is very good with adult bar mitzvahs.

JOEY: Do you know who I am?

MICHAEL: Ben Goldman's grandfather.

JOEY: I can't be in Benny's class. I'll study with you.

MICHAEL: I don't teach bar mitzvah class.

JOEY: I can't go to the same class as Benny.

MICHAEL: The Schara Tzedeck has special adult classes. They're a lot bigger than we are and—

JOEY: It has to be here.

MICHAEL: You've already waited a while for your bar mitzvah. I'm sure you can wait a bit longer.

JOEY: What kind of donation would help out?

MICHAEL: Every little bit helps.

JOEY: And a big bit helps a lot more.

MICHAEL: You'll love bar mitzvah class, Mr. Brant.

JOEY: Call me Joey.

MICHAEL: Mr. Brant, how long has it been since you've been to shul?

JOEY: It's Friday?

MICHAEL: Yes.

JOEY: Fifty-two years . . . Give or take.

MICHAEL: Stay tonight. I'll buy you a glass of wine.

JOEY: Is it kosher?

MICHAEL: Yes. Sorry about that.

JOEY: What do they do to get all the flavour out—circumcise the grapes?

MICHAEL: I'm sure kosher wines are a lot better than the last time you were in shul. And after service we have carrot cake. And schnapps.

JOEY: I have poker.

MICHAEL: You know what they say, Mr. Brant. Know when to hold 'em, know when to fold 'em.

JOEY: I've heard that.

MICHAEL: Book of Kenny Rogers. Verse two.

JOEY: Are you sure you're a rabbi?

MICHAEL: If you're really serious about this—

JOEY: I am.

MICHAEL: Know when to walk away. Now I really need to shower. I'll get Sheryl to enrol you in class.

She exits to shower, leaving JOEY. *He goes back to studying the books on her shelf. He picks up the phone to use the intercom.*

JOEY: Sheryl? You're still there? . . . Good. Yes, yes . . . yesssss. Joey Brant . . .

Rabbi Michael wants me to book in for a bar mitzvah class next week. Thanks. Yes. She's fine. Tell the security guard he won't need his taser.

SCENE THREE

BIMAH

Friday night.

MICHAEL *is behind the podium delivering her sermon to our audience—the congregation. She's now wearing a tallis and head covering.*

MICHAEL: Every Shabbat we all come together to celebrate our blessings—as individuals, as families and as a community. And, of course, it's a blessing to help this synagogue.

As we stand here tonight, celebrating this bat mitzvah, I'd like to remind you about the fundraising dinner next month for our renovation project, to bring our auditorium in line with the new building code. And now, to lead us in Adon Olam, our bat mitzvah girl, Leslie-Ann Shapiro-Wong.

MICHAEL *walks off stage.*

JOEY *is watching. From the house. As he exits our focus shifts.*

SCENE FOUR

RABBI'S OFFICE

The following Tuesday.

MICHAEL is at her desk. On the phone. Civvies. Head covered.

MICHAEL: I'll be there, honey. Of course, I'll be there . . . I had a funeral. You know I would have been there if I could have been. I'm sorry.

The intercom buzzes. MICHAEL looks saved.

Just one second.

She clicks the intercom.

SHERYL: It's Mr. Brant. I told him he had to wait but—

MICHAEL: It's all right, Sheryl.

She switches back to the phone.

We can't afford it. I know. Yes, I know. You can pick me up at nine. She knows I'd be there if I could.

JOEY is at the door in his everyday outfit.

Love you.

She spots JOEY and acknowledges that she's seen him.

Of course, I'll be there.

She hangs up.

Come in.

JOEY: Ten years? Fifteen?

MICHAEL: Sorry?

JOEY: That didn't sound like a conversation between newlyweds. Fourteen years, am I right?

MICHAEL: (*surprised*) Thirteen.

JOEY: It's a gift.

MICHAEL: I don't need your services.

JOEY: So you do know who I am? Sandee talked about me?

MICHAEL: I read the papers.

JOEY: Is that why you wanted to see me? I've never worked for a rabbi before. Everyone thinks it's the seven-year itch, but that's just the name of a movie.

Thirteen, thirteen is tough. And how old is your husband?

He looks around.

I should have known you were married—but no photos.

MICHAEL: We met at yeshiva.

JOEY: Same age?

MICHAEL: I'm two years older.

He shakes his head, "Not good."

JOEY: So first marriage then. How many kids?

MICHAEL: One daughter.

JOEY: Thirteen is tough.

MICHAEL: Daniel and I are fine.

JOEY: I'm sure you are. But if you ever want to talk, it's on the house. Is he a rabbi too?

MICHAEL: I heard about your class.

JOEY: So he dropped out because you got better grades?

MICHAEL: He got better grades. He was more interested in the philosophy than the practice. I was more interested in the practice.

JOEY: He doesn't like people.

MICHAEL: He doesn't like politics. Your class.

JOEY: So is this the principal's office?

MICHAEL: Congratulations. I didn't know Ari, Cantor Reuben, could get that angry.

JOEY: It wasn't my fault.

MICHAEL: Of course not.

JOEY: I told you I couldn't take a class with all those kids.

MICHAEL: So you sent them all for pizza during the break.

JOEY: When Sandee's little league team won a game, we'd always go for pizza. When they lost we'd go for pizza too—just not the good stuff. We lost, it was one of those chains that figures if they give you extra cheese you won't notice how bad the pizza is.

MICHAEL: You sent them alone.

JOEY: It was just across the street. I had my girl take them.

MICHAEL: Hawaiian pizza.

JOEY: It's my favourite.

MICHAEL: You know what's on a Hawaiian pizza?

JOEY: Poi?

MICHAEL: Ari is furious.

JOEY: What's wrong with a little pineapple?

MICHAEL: Three of those kids keep kosher.

JOEY: Not anymore . . . Tell them it was beef. And soy cheese. And that it was gluten free.

(*off her glare*) If G-d had known about Hawaiian pizza, there would have been loopholes in this whole kosher thing.

MICHAEL: Their parents are furious.

JOEY: They told their parents? Little snitches. Serves 'em right if they're in trouble.

MICHAEL: Cantor Reuben told them.

JOEY: Of course he did. What was he thinking?

MICHAEL: I'm really not sure.

JOEY: I can't do this in front of Benny. I'm his zayda. It's not right. I couldn't even tell him why I was in class.

MICHAEL: You can go to another shul. There are other shuls, other rabbis. I'd be happy to introduce you to the Lubavitchers or—

JOEY: No. It has to be here.

MICHAEL: I'll ask him to teach you privately.

JOEY: He told me if he ever saw me outside of shul again he'd call the police.

MICHAEL: The police?

JOEY: I'm sure he was just being funny but . . .

MICHAEL: He has no sense of humour.

JOEY: You're kidding.

MICHAEL: If I was, he'd never know it. I'm sorry, that's not fair. I'm sure he has a sense of humour, but he's Russian. They think Chekhov is funny.

JOEY: I prefer Spock and Bones.

MICHAEL: My husband's Russian too.

JOEY: So you married him because he makes you laugh?

MICHAEL: He's funnier than Cantor Reuben.

JOEY: I should hope so. Isn't there some way we can just do this and not make a thing out of it?

MICHAEL: You want a bar mitzvah . . . and I'm guessing you're a little past your thirteenth birthday. If you're willing to skip a few poker games and come Fridays . . .

JOEY: If I have to.

Can I come Thursdays?

MICHAEL: If you don't mind being the only one here. The only time we make minyan on Thursday is when someone dies. And even then . . .

JOEY: So much for poker night.

MICHAEL: Want to tell me why?

JOEY: I was serious about that donation.

MICHAEL: Maybe after your big day.

JOEY: I bought a table at the fundraising dinner.

MICHAEL: A table? Thank you.

JOEY: What if I pay you to tutor me?

MICHAEL: I can find someone else to teach you. Our old rabbi—Rabbi Solomon—he's retired, but I can ask him.

JOEY: I don't want everyone to know. I don't want anyone to know.

JOEY pulls out his chequebook.

How much would you charge for a few classes?

MICHAEL: I'm very busy.

JOEY: For the shul. For the renovations.

He presents her with a cheque.

MICHAEL: I'm really sorry, Mr. Brant, but—

JOEY: So the cantor can buy the kids kosher pizza.

MICHAEL: It's not easy to get kosher pizza around here.

JOEY: I know a guy.

MICHAEL: That's . . . a lot of pizza.

JOEY: What's it going to take to make this happen?

MICHAEL: Some bar mitzvahs are booked years in advance. If you want a Saturday service so you can have family and friends—

JOEY: What day does nobody show up?

MICHAEL: That would be . . . most of them.

JOEY: You pick a day, I'll make it work.

MICHAEL: Do you want a big reception? I'm assuming we don't need kosher catering.

JOEY: No reception. No guests. Just you and me is fine.

MICHAEL: This isn't a Vegas wedding. We still need ten adults for the service. You know what a minyan is?

JOEY: Yeah, the crackers we eat for Passover. Yes, I know what a minyan is. Ten men is fine.

MICHAEL: Or ten women. That's okay here.

JOEY: I had dreams like that when I was younger.

MICHAEL: No guests. No reception. So who are we doing this for?

JOEY: Benny.

MICHAEL: So you want him to see—

JOEY: No. No. You can't tell Benny. I told him I was just there to sit in. I asked the cantor not to say anything.

MICHAEL: Mr. Brant, all bar mitzvah means is that you're thirteen. You've already accomplished that. The ceremony is a celebration of that milestone—but it's all the same in the eyes of G-d and the community whether you have a ceremony or not.

JOEY: It doesn't feel the same.

MICHAEL: If you just want to stand up and have me say you're bar mitzvahed I can call you to the Torah anytime.

JOEY: I want to do this properly. Like the Chinese girl the other night.

MICHAEL: She's Jewish.

JOEY: Yeah, more Jewish than me. She had a bat mitzvah. I want to do everything the kids do. I want to do this right. And I need to do this before Benny does his.

MICHAEL: What about the Thursday before?

JOEY: Thank you.

MICHAEL: You seriously want to do this? If I give you homework— If you're serious about this . . .

JOEY: If you give me homework, I'll do homework. But no Cantor Putin.

MICHAEL: I need to know if I ask you to do something, you'll do it.

JOEY: Can I smoke during recess?

MICHAEL doesn't laugh.

Are you sure you're not Russian?

MICHAEL: If you skip a class, if you don't do your homework, if you waste my time, you can still do this, I'll still keep the night for you, but you can go back to Cantor Putin.

JOEY: I'll be here.

MICHAEL: Thursday nights?

JOEY: I can do Thursdays.

MICHAEL: And if you can't skip poker nights, a few Saturday mornings. How's your Hebrew?

JOEY: Rusty.

MICHAEL: Do you know your aleph bet?

JOEY: I used to.

MICHAEL: It's like riding a bike. It'll come back to you.

JOEY: I haven't been on a bike in a while.

MICHAEL: Let me get you something.

She searches her shelves.

JOEY: Please tell me it's not a bike.

She starts checking her files.

MICHAEL: This'll help.

She hands him a book on learning Judaism.

JOEY: Thank you.

MICHAEL: I use it for conversion class. It covers everything you need to know. So what do you want to do for your bar mitzvah? We can make it very basic if you want—an aliyah, a few prayers.

JOEY: Whatever Benny's doing.

MICHAEL: Benny's probably leading a few prayers, reading the haftorah. And he'll do a short sermon.

JOEY: In English, right?

MICHAEL: Yes. I'm assuming stage fright isn't an issue for you.

JOEY: Not since I was Benny's age.

MICHAEL: Okay, we'll make this work.

JOEY: What kind of speech do the kids do?

MICHAEL: I can show you a few. They always give me copies.

JOEY: Yeah, I'd like to see 'em.

She hands him another book.

MICHAEL: To freshen up on your Hebrew.

He hands over the cheque.

JOEY: Your tutoring fee.

MICHAEL: I can't . . . Mr. Brant.

But he's already on his way out.

JOEY: See you Thursday.

MICHAEL: Mr. Brant.

She considers the cheque, considers tearing it, stops, then puts it in her desk.

SCENE FIVE

JOEY'S OFFICE

A few days before classes.

JOEY *recites Adon Olam perfectly to the Gerovitch tune.*

JOEY: Adon olam, asher malach, b'terem kol y'tzir nivra. L'et na'asah v'cheftzo kol, azai melech sh'mo nikra.

Like riding a bike.

And now . . . all stumbles.

Vakrew kilo hako—

He tries again.

Vakra keyhole. Vakray . . .

Shit.

SCENE SIX

RABBI'S OFFICE

The following Thursday—first class.

MICHAEL *is at her desk, prepared to teach, as* JOEY *enters.*

JOEY: "Today I am a man." "Today I am a man." All the speeches begin with "today I am a man." Maybe . . . today I am a grandfather.

MICHAEL: The kids love that part. You don't have to say it.

JOEY: What else do you have?

He starts looking through her books.

MICHAEL: You really don't have to make a speech.

JOEY: A lot of books.

MICHAEL: There are a lot of books about being Jewish. Jews like to write. Just talk about why you're here, I'm sure there's a story. Waiting, what, fifty years to get called to the Torah.

JOEY: Give or take.

MICHAEL: There's got to be a story.

JOEY finds a book. Grins.

JOEY: This is a sex book.

MICHAEL: *Kosher Sex.*

JOEY: Shmuley Bow-teach. Sounds kinky.

She corrects his pronunciation.

MICHAEL: Boteach.

It's a name, not a position.

Just speak from the heart, say why you want to do this. That can be your speech. You don't even have to write it.

JOEY: And this one . . .

He wolf whistles.

What are you doing with the Kama Sutra?

MICHAEL: I counsel people. I counsel couples. It's part of the job.

JOEY: It has pictures.

MICHAEL: Of course it has pictures. I'm a rabbi, not a priest.

JOEY: If they had pictures like this when I was in Hebrew school I might have stuck around for my bar mitzvah.

MICHAEL: I can't talk to you about sex, Joey. It wouldn't be right.

JOEY: Too embarrassing?

MICHAEL: You're not a man yet.

JOEY: I've seen things on the Internet.

MICHAEL: I'm sure you have.

JOEY: The girl you were talking to after services . . . The one with the pink prayer book. Cancer?

MICHAEL: Yeah.

JOEY: Shit. She's the one—

MICHAEL: What one?

JOEY: Benny told me about her. That must be . . . I can only imagine.

MICHAEL: What did Benny tell you?

JOEY: There was a kid his age in shul. Said that's how he knew there was no G-d. What was I supposed to tell him?

MICHAEL: Let's work on your Hebrew. How'd the homework go?

JOEY: She's praying? Or are her parents making her show up? I get why they'd show up, but the kid . . . Why not just let her play video games or hang out with her friends?

MICHAEL: If we can do the aleph bet today.

JOEY: The cancer kid. She's praying?

MICHAEL: Every Shabbat.

JOEY: I'd find a different G-d.

MICHAEL: Who? Thor?

JOEY: At least he's buff. Girls like that.

MICHAEL: I'll suggest it to her.

JOEY: She's here every week?

MICHAEL: Yeah.

JOEY: What . . . what do you do with that?

MICHAEL: Thor? Not too much. But, you're right, he is buff.

JOEY: Death. Cancer. Shit like that. Do you really just tell people it'll all be fine because G-d has a plan? Is that what you tell kids?

MICHAEL: I mostly just listen. With death we're supposed to listen. We're never supposed to say "I understand," because that's impossible.

JOEY: I want to believe in G-d, in Heaven in . . . this . . . but I see things like that, what do I tell Benny? When Sandee's cat died I told her we gave it to farmers.

MICHAEL: There are some things no one really understands. That's what shiva's all about. Have you been to a shiva?

JOEY: Too many.

MICHAEL: You offer the family food. You listen if they want to talk. You pray. The whole community goes for a week and then, by the end of the week—

JOEY: The family's sick of visitors.

MICHAEL: That's the point.

JOEY: Seriously?

MICHAEL: It helps you move on.

JOEY: My father, when he went to shiva, he always said . . . Zeek room latka.

MICHAEL: Zikhrono livrakha. It basically means, "May his memory be a blessing."

JOEY: I like that.

MICHAEL: Or you say, "Alav ha shalom."

JOEY: Shalom. Hello, goodbye, peace. Alava?

MICHAEL: Upon him. Peace be upon him.

JOEY: I like the other one.

MICHAEL: Me too. We don't usually get into this for bar mitzvah classes, but if you want to talk about shiva, I'm okay with that.

JOEY: What do you tell a kid like that girl?

MICHAEL: Rachel . . . She's my daughter.

JOEY: Fuck.

MICHAEL: Yeah.

So I tell her she needs to keep taking her medicine, even when it makes her feel sicker. I tell her to trust the doctors. I tell her, her daddy and I love her.

JOEY: Shit. I'm sorry. I didn't—

MICHAEL: It's okay. She's been sick a long time. I'm used to it.

The four least reassuring words in the English language—"It's probably not cancer."

I should have just told you. I thought you knew. I had pictures of her and Daniel in the office but ... this ... kept happening. Someone would see her picture and say, "What am I doing talking to you about my problems?"

And then they'd get that look you have now.

Or they'd cry.

JOEY: I'm so sorry. The Thor thing ...

MICHAEL: She'll love it. I should get her a poster. And if she wanted to spend Shabbat playing video games or watching TV, I'd let her. But she's the one who bought that pink cover for her Bible so it wouldn't look like everyone else's. Pretty sure she likes it here better than I do. She likes staring at the ner tamid.

JOEY looks at her blankly.

The eternal flame.

My favourite concept in Judaism—tikkun olam. You know it?

JOEY: Like Adon Olam?

MICHAEL: Adon means "G-d."

Olam—"world or universe."

Tikkun is repair.

Tikkun olam. "Repair of the world." Kindness for the sake of creating a better world.

Since everybody takes yoga these days, whenever I talk about it in shul somebody asks afterwards if it's like the Jewish equivalent of karma. I tell them karma is more like the Hindi version of tikkun olam. Put good into the world, the world gets better. But karma comes with a warning label—whatever you do will come back at you. That's a principle of Wicca too.

Tikkun olam is doing good for the sake of goodness based on the principle that goodness makes the world better. Rachel still believes. With all her heart.

JOEY: So she believes there's a plan?

MICHAEL: That there's something more. Something greater than us. Something worth believing in. Maybe you can tell that to Benny . . .

And that's why there are no photos of them in here. This is your session, not mine.

JOEY: So the guy with your daughter . . . That's your husband?

MICHAEL: Daniel.

JOEY: He's pretty buff too. Not Thor buff . . .

MICHAEL: Russian. Good peasant stock. Where are you at with the aleph bet?

He reads from the book.

JOEY: Aleph, bet, gimmel, dalath, he, vav, zay . . . Rabbi?

MICHAEL is elsewhere.

MICHAEL: Zayin.

JOEY: Zayin.

MICHAEL: Like riding a bike.

JOEY: Het, tet, yod, kaf.

SCENE SEVEN

BIMAH

Friday night: Shavuot.

MICHAEL: When I was growing up, my favourite holiday was Shavuot. I've always loved to stay up late. I've always loved to study. And on Shavuot, that's what we do . . . we stay up all night . . . and we talk about Torah. About the creation of the earth, and what we believe, and why.

It was a chance to ask questions about . . .

Anything we wanted to know.

I remember one Shavuot talking about the creation of the universe and how G-d's clock didn't work the same way as ours did and how the dinosaurs were here for millions of years before we showed up. I always thought it was the perfect holiday, the celebration of being chosen.

Moses would speak and G-d would answer him with a voice. I would try to imagine that conversation, that voice. And I hoped, like I think we all do at some point in our lives, that one day I would speak and G-d would answer me.

One Shavuot, late at night, when most of the adults had decided to nap, I asked my rabbi if this ever happens, if there was a way to make it happen. We all pray, we all talk to G-d, did he ever talk back to us? And I remember my rabbi's answer. "G-d already spoke and he already answered when he gave us the gift of the Ten Commandments." I was afraid to tell the rabbi that what I really wanted to ask G-d was whether Bradley Wolfe would ever ask me out.

SCENE EIGHT

RABBI'S OFFICE

The following Thursday.

JOEY and MICHAEL enter together.

MICHAEL: Let's work on tefillin tonight. Roll up your sleeve.

She indicates the correct arm for JOEY.

That one.

He rolls up his sleeve. The tefillin are on the desk.

JOEY: I expected more people.

MICHAEL: Not bad for Shavuot.

JOEY: It's a big holiday, right. I remember more people. Rachel and Daniel weren't here.

MICHAEL: You probably just came for high holidays. Unless you're left-handed you want to use your left arm.

She starts wrapping the tefillin for him.

Most people just come for high holidays.

JOEY: We came every Shabbat.

MICHAEL: I guess more people showed up before they invented the talkies.

JOEY: So now it's a spiritual ER. High holidays. Funerals. Weddings.

MICHAEL: And bar mitzvahs . . .

Different people need different things.

JOEY: There was something you said . . . about creation . . . how it was millions of years, not seven days.

MICHAEL: You haven't heard of evolution? Flex. Close to the heart.

She continues placing the tefillin.

JOEY: When I was a kid it was seven days. Sorry, six. And then the Lord rested.

MICHAEL: Still is. But you know that's a metaphor, right. Hold. Now you say the blessing.

Baruch atah adonai eloheinu me-lech ha-olam ah-sher keed-shanu b'mitz-vo-tav vetsee-vahnu l'ho-niach tefillin.

JOEY: Amein. You're a rabbi. Aren't you supposed to believe?

MICHAEL: It's the twenty-first century. And the big bang makes more sense than *The Flintstones*. Wrap twice in the upper arm. Seven lower.

JOEY: I thought believing in the Bible was part of the job description.

MICHAEL: I believe in the teachings behind the stories. That's what the stories are for—that's what most stories are for. Do you think Jonah spent three days surfing around in a whale?

JOEY: What about . . . other rabbis? Orthodox rabbis?

MICHAEL: Now put this on your head. Head and heart—to bind our minds and emotions to G-d.

JOEY puts on the headpiece.

My dad thought they were metaphors. He was orthodox.

JOEY: What did your dad do?

MICHAEL: He was a rabbi back in the old country.

JOEY: Russia?

MICHAEL: Los Angeles. Mom runs a gallery. My grandfather was a rabbi in the Ukraine.

JOEY: And what did he believe?

MICHAEL: That he needed to get out of the Ukraine before the Cossacks killed him.

JOEY: Did he believe in metaphors?

MICHAEL: I never got to ask him.

JOEY: The Cossacks? I'm sorry. So you never met him?

MICHAEL: He lived with us till I was ten, refused to learn English, just Russian and Yiddish. I learned just enough Yiddish to know when he thought Dad was being a schmuck.

So we never had any great theological discussions.

The headpiece is set.

And now the second prayer. Baruch atah adonai eloheinu me-lech ha-olam ah-sher keed-shanu b'mitz-vo-tav vetsee-vahnu al mitzvat tefillin.

JOEY: Amein.

A third generation rabbi.

MICHAEL: Does that make you feel better? Am I more official now—even though I'm . . . young?

JOEY: The burning bush? Eden? Noah? All metaphors?

MICHAEL: I always thought the burning bush was too weird to be a metaphor. And not all that poetic. I figured that might have happened.

JOEY: I thought religion was about faith. Aren't all Jews supposed to believe these things?

MICHAEL: We can believe in G-d and not believe Noah somehow rounded up breeding pairs of giraffes and gophers and chipmunks in the forests of Gomorrah. Metaphors, parables, stories, fairy tales. What matters is the message at the heart of them.

JOEY: You don't think it matters if they're true?

MICHAEL: They're all true.

JOEY: So does that mean you don't believe in miracles?

MICHAEL: Miracles happen every day. Now you get it around the hand. It should look like the letter shin.

And they start to wrap the hand.

JOEY: Real miracles. Bible miracles. Parting the Red Sea. Plagues of locusts. Feeding the masses with loaves and fishes.

MICHAEL: You know that last one isn't one of ours, right? Otherwise, you're going back to Hebrew school.

JOEY: Ten Commandment miracles. Moses miracles.

MICHAEL: Do you think they're true?

JOEY: I'm not a rabbi. I thought it was your job to believe so I didn't have to.

I want to know someone has faith.

Is G-d a metaphor?

MICHAEL: I have faith. My father had faith. My grandfather . . . he knew how to read, so he became the town's rabbi.

What do you believe?

JOEY: Never draw to an inside straight. Never play poker with a man named Doc. And there's no such thing as an amicable divorce.

MICHAEL: From the Bible.

JOEY: All of it. None of it. But I thought all of it was supposed to be true. That the people who wrote it believed it was true.

MICHAEL: Maybe they did. Take the hand and once around the middle finger, bottom part of the knuckle—

He puts forward the wrong knuckle and she adjusts his hand.

This knuckle. Like the letter shin.

And they wrap the knuckles, etc.

That's it. Top part and then wrap.

JOEY: Stylish. And now I get in the boxing ring.

MICHAEL: Maybe they just knew a good story and took the most powerful images from every culture they encountered. If the stories weren't good we wouldn't still be telling them.

JOEY: So are you a rabbi because it's the family business?

MICHAEL: I wanted to help people.

JOEY: And fireman was taken?

MICHAEL: I've always loved it. I loved watching my father in shul, watching him help people, thinking . . . that's my dad. The shul always felt more like home than home.

I loved it the way Rachel does.

Any shul anywhere in the world always feels like home. The Torahs . . . I always loved the ceremony around the Torahs. The feel, the smell, the love for the Word . . .

Why do you do what you do? Why not some other kind of law?

JOEY: You mean something more respectable?

MICHAEL: Just trying to picture you as a boy dreaming . . . quarterback, policeman, astronaut . . . no . . . divorce lawyer.

JOEY: If I could have been Batman, that would have been my first choice.

MICHAEL: So when you realized Batman was taken you thought . . . someone has to negotiate alimony?

JOEY: First year law we had a speaker come to class. He talks about divorce law and he tells us, "It's like going to the roulette table and betting on black, or more like . . . being the house. It's not like love even triumphs fifty percent of the time." And he was right.

People I don't see: some are happy—G-d bless their simple souls. Some make compromises. They forgive the unforgivable.

They live without love. Or they come up with a new definition—one that no longer includes passion or sex or talking to each other over breakfast.

I'm in the same business as you are. I help people through their pain.

MICHAEL: We're not in the same business.

JOEY: Maybe not. With the law . . . no metaphors. The words in my books . . . I have to take them literally.

MICHAEL: Now we unwrap it—arm first—you try.

He starts to unwrap.

You want to unwrap in the same order you put it on.

JOEY takes the tefillin off and then practices placing the tefillin again himself.

I'm guessing you didn't take Tzeporah to shul. So her mom?

JOEY: Sandee. We raised her with no religion at all. Her mother and I . . . we agreed that if she wanted religion—

If she wanted religion she could decide for herself when she was older. So no shul, no bat mitzvah.

Like this?

MICHAEL: Good. Tighter.

JOEY: Then Sandee goes on a trip to Jerusalem after high school and when she comes back . . . she's changed her name, gone orthodox and wants to make aliyah.

MICHAEL: You must have been so proud.

JOEY: Her mother thinks this is great. A direction.

At this point we'd been split for years or this would have done it. Me. I want to call in those leg-breakers who deprogram Hare Krishnas. No offence.

MICHAEL: Why would I be offended? You think I'm a cult leader. No offence to the Krishnas.

JOEY: I think to qualify as a cult leader you need more people to show up for services.

> MICHAEL *adjusts the tefillin on his head. Tight.*

Ow . . .

She doesn't make aliyah but marries that Israeli schmuck instead. And then Benny comes along.

And now I'm always hearing how I denied her a religious upbringing—and how I'd never even told her about my bar mitzvah.

MICHAEL: You had a bar mitzvah? I thought—

JOEY: No—she thinks I had a bar mitzvah. Here. All these years I've never lied to her. But Benny asks . . .

MICHAEL: And you lied to him.

JOEY: And he tells his mom and he tells her my bar mitzvah was here. So now it's a family tradition.

His tefillin are on properly.

MICHAEL: You've got it. So that's why she's doing the bar mitzvah here.

JOEY: Tradition. For me.

He starts to unwrap the tefillin.

So I'll go back to shul.

MICHAEL: Why did you stop going to shul?

JOEY: I grew up.

MICHAEL: Do you remember what the tefillin symbolize?

JOEY: S&M . . .

Tradition.

Feel free to add some Fiddler *flair.*

Like everything else we do.

MICHAEL: You realize there are verses from the Torah in here.

JOEY: The original Cracker Jack box.

MICHAEL: Connecting our head and our heart. Box on the head, box on the heart. Sounds very new age, doesn't it? And it's about remembering that G-d brought us out of Egypt.

JOEY: I thought it was about showing the goyim we're Jewish, so they know who to beat up at school.

He finishes unwrapping the tefillin, kisses them and puts them away.

MICHAEL: That too.

So Benny thinks you had a bar mitzvah here. So you're having your bar mitzvah here.

JOEY: If you really don't believe G-d made everything in six days. Noah. The Red Sea. What do you believe?

MICHAEL: I believe in G-d. And I believe those stories, those metaphors, the parables—they show us a way through the world.

JOEY starts for the door.

JOEY: See you next week.

MICHAEL: We've got a yahrzeit next Thursday—I need to make a minyan. Would you come early and lead us in one of the prayers?

JOEY: Do I have a choice?

MICHAEL: It'll help you prepare and—

MICHAEL's phone rings.

I should—

JOEY: I'll be there.

MICHAEL grabs the phone.

MICHAEL: Rachel, is everything . . . it's in the freezer. You can just microwave it.

Don't worry, I'll be there soon. I promise.

SCENE NINE

JOEY'S OFFICE

Between classes.

JOEY: (*reading*) Y'hei sh'mei raba m'varach l'alam ul'almei almaya.

He puts the book down—he knows this by heart.

Yitbarach v'yishtabach, v'yitpa'ar v'yitromam v'yitnaseh, v'yithadar v'yit'aleh v'yit'halal sh'mei d'kud'sha, b'rich hu.

This is bringing up memories. Not great memories.

L'eila min-kol-birchata v'shirata, tushb'chata v'nechemata da'amiran b'alma, v'im'ru: amein. Y'hei shlama raba min-sh'maya v'chayim aleinu v'al-kol-yisrael, v'im'ru: amein.

Our focus shifts, and JOEY seamlessly finishes the prayer in MICHAEL's office, the following Thursday.

SCENE TEN

RABBI'S OFFICE

JOEY: Oseh shalom bim'ro'mah, hu ya'say shalom aleinu v'al kol yisroel v'imru amein.

MICHAEL: That one's hard to forget.

JOEY: Said it too many times for too many people. I don't know how you do it.

MICHAEL: It's in the job description. Let's work on your Torah portion.

JOEY: I get to do it in Hebrew and English?

MICHAEL: Hebrew first, then English, then the sermon. But let's start with the English to get the sense of it.

JOEY: And it came to pass after these things, that G-d did prove Abraham, and said unto him, Abraham. And he said, Here am I. And he said, Take now thy son, thine only son, whom thou lovest, even Isaac, and get thee into the land of Moriah. And offer him there for a burnt offering upon—

I'm sure it makes more sense in Hebrew.

MICHAEL: Thoughts on Abraham?

JOEY: He would have been great with al-Qaeda.

What kind of asshole is ready to kill his son because he hears voices?

The kind of person who flies planes into buildings.

MICHAEL: He knew G-d was speaking to him.

JOEY: So did Charlie Manson.

MICHAEL's not amused.

So it was right for him not to question?

MICHAEL: It was faith.

JOEY: In a mysterious voice that already told him to cut off part of his son's schmeckel. Like that wasn't crazy enough.

Is there any chance our whole religion is based on a paranoid schizophrenic who was playing his ancient Beatles album backwards? No offence.

MICHAEL: Of course not.

JOEY: What kind of parent does that? Would you kill your child for—oh shit, I'm sorry.

MICHAEL: You're right, you win. It's all bullshit.

JOEY: I didn't mean—

MICHAEL: Yeah, you did. Look beyond the story. That's what we do in the Talmud, in all the interpretations. Not what does it say, what does it mean? It's all metaphor, right. What's the metaphor?

JOEY: That faith is rewarded with a son who will need therapy for the rest of his life? And this is why so many of our people need shrinks?

MICHAEL: If you want to wait and do another portion—

JOEY: I'm a lawyer, I can act like this makes sense to me. Does faith make you feel better?

MICHAEL: It makes Rachel feel better.

JOEY: And you?

MICHAEL: We're not talking about me.

JOEY: I'm trying to understand faith. I'm not big on trusting people I can see. Trusting a mysterious voice . . . even if you weren't going through . . . what you're going through . . . I'd want to know.

MICHAEL: I know there's something beyond us.

JOEY: And . . . that's enough for you?

MICHAEL: I'd prefer if the chemo was doing its job. But yes—I don't think G-d is intervening in every life and choosing the winning side in every baseball game—but I believe there's a G-d and that things happen for a reason.

JOEY: I have an easier time believing G-d bets on baseball.

MICHAEL: Now in Hebrew. We need to teach you how to sing this.

JOEY: And Rachel really believes?

MICHAEL: With all her heart.

She follows this thread, starting as the conversation with JOEY *and continuing as her sermon at the bimah . . .*

SCENE ELEVEN

BIMAH

Friday night.

MICHAEL: When my daughter Rachel was old enough to ask questions, the first question she asked at shul was about this light, the ner tamid, our eternal light.

She loves the idea that every synagogue everywhere in the world has one.

It wasn't the Torah that excited her, but the light above the ark that holds the Torah. She wanted to know . . .

Why does it burn forever?

I told her it was because there was a lamp in the ancient temple that was always lit and that it was a symbol that G-d is always there, and that G-d and our belief are eternal.

For Rachel it's not the symbolism that appeals to her, it's the light itself. It doesn't matter that it's just an orange bulb, every time we visit a shul that's the first thing she wants to see.

She needs to know that the shul has a light, that it is on, that the light will always be there.

JOEY watches. As MICHAEL exits, JOEY watches the light.

SCENE TWELVE

RABBI'S OFFICE

The following Thursday.

MICHAEL *is in her office. Alone. It takes a moment before we realize . . . She's smoking something . . . A joint. She's been crying.* JOEY *arrives, sees her. She doesn't see him. She's looking at the wall with her diplomas/art/photos/keepsakes.*

MICHAEL: Shit.

JOEY: Rabbis are allowed to swear?

MICHAEL: Check the commandments. We're not supposed to take the Lord's name in vain. So unless you think the Lord is shit, shit is fine. Fuck is okay too. But G dash D damn, not so much.

JOEY: Shit.

MICHAEL: Exactly. I didn't think we were supposed to swear either. Sorry, Joey, I forgot it was Thursday. Not this week, okay?

JOEY: What is it?

MICHAEL: Nothing, I'm great.

JOEY: I didn't think rabbis did this either.

MICHAEL: It's medicinal. For the cancer.

JOEY: I didn't know they'd prescribe to kids.

MICHAEL: They don't. Can't risk them getting any bad habits. And smoking causes cancer . . .

It helps.

JOEY: You?

MICHAEL: Rachel. It helps her appetite and, when we're lucky, it makes her laugh.

JOEY: I've got glaucoma. And I own four Grateful Dead albums.

MICHAEL: As long as it's medicinal.

She offers the joint to JOEY.

JOEY: Holy shit.

MICHAEL: Dealers save the good stuff for cancer kids.

JOEY: How is she?

MICHAEL: She's great. She's going to a better place.

JOEY: I'm sorry . . . I thought . . .

MICHAEL: Yeah, so did I.

JOEY: How, no, forget it.

MICHAEL: How long does she have? How long have I known? A month, maybe two.

The pediatric oncologist says if she's really lucky she'll make it to her birthday—nine weeks.

So we can give her a bat mitzvah just before we bury her. How long have I known? I've always known. I still don't know. I'm supposed to believe in miracles, I'm just not supposed to pray for them.

JOEY: I'm so sorry. I know I'm not supposed to say that, but I am so sorry.

MICHAEL: How's your reading coming?

JOEY: You want me to read now?

MICHAEL: You're here. I'm here.

The intercom crackles.

SHERYL: Rabbi, I'm going home now. Is everything all right?

MICHAEL and JOEY react to the interruption.

MICHAEL: Thank you, Sheryl, have a nice night.

JOEY: Does she know what you're doing in here?

MICHAEL: Very rarely. Now, shall we—

MICHAEL hands JOEY a prayer book.

JOEY: Can I do a prayer?

MICHAEL: Dealer's choice.

JOEY sings—the old tune.

JOEY: Adon olam, asher malach, b'terem kol y'tzir nivra. L'et na'asah v'cheftzo kol, azai melech sh'mo nikra—

MICHAEL: Not bad. But that's not the tune we use anymore.

JOEY: They changed the tune? They're not supposed to change the tunes.

MICHAEL: So that means we won't do the version of Adon Olam set to "Hallelujah" or the song from *Hamilton.*

JOEY: You're joking.

MICHAEL sings to tune of "You'll Be Back."

MICHAEL: Adon olam. Asher malach.

JOEY: Is nothing sacred?

MICHAEL: Broadway copyright. I'm guessing if we went with the *Hamilton* version we'd need one of your colleagues to defend the shul.

I'll record the music for the version we use.

And you need to work your ch-es. Like "kkhhh." You need to sound more like—

She takes out another joint. Lights it.

JOEY: An old Jew waking up with a throat full of phlegm the morning after smoking a joint?

MICHAEL: That'd do it.

JOEY: (*overemphasizing his "ch-es"*) Adon olam, asher malach, b'terem kol y'tzir nivra. L'et na'asah v'cheftzo kol, azai melech sh'mo nikra.

MICHAEL: Not bad.

JOEY: Maybe if I get high for the ceremony.

MICHAEL: You wouldn't be the first bar mitzvah boy who found a way to take the edge off. It used to be wine. Kosher wine. This is an improvement.

JOEY: Today I am a dude.

MICHAEL: Today I am a dude.

And the stoned kids—always better than the drunk kids.

My first year as a rabbi, I had one girl throw up on the bimah. I told everyone it was nerves because I didn't want to ruin her big day, but Sarah's nerves sure smelled like Manischewitz.

JOEY: That's, that's just—

MICHAEL: Vile. Worst smell ever.

JOEY: Holy shit.

MICHAEL: The holy part is probably sacrilegious. The stoned kids usually just giggle a lot.

JOEY: (*giggling*) I'm already worrying about people laughing.

MICHAEL: No one's going to laugh. You'll be fine.

JOEY: But my Hebrew—I keep getting the words wrong.

MICHAEL: It's a bar mitzvah, not the entrance exam for yeshiva. No one cares if you say the words right. No one's going to know . . .

Okay, I'll know. The cantor will know. And all the old guys with the crazy eyebrows.

JOEY: I resemble that remark.

MICHAEL: Yes, Mr. Posner will know. If he has his hearing aid on. None of your friends will know.

Just say it like you know what the words mean and as long as I don't wince everyone will assume you got it right.

I conducted last week's service entirely in Greek. No one had a clue.

JOEY: Greek?

MICHAEL laughs.

MICHAEL: I should try it sometime just to see what happens. Instead of the Torah portion I should just read a passage from an Israeli magazine.

See if Mr. Posner is listening.

JOEY: I want to do it right.

MICHAEL: It's not a pass–fail thing. You show up, you pass.

JOEY: I don't just want a participation ribbon.

MICHAEL: I can get you the gold. I know a guy. So why are we doing this, Joey?

JOEY: Benny.

MICHAEL: People lie to me all the time. Usually I'm okay with that. You wanna stay here tonight, no bullshit. How'd you escape a bar mitzvah?

JOEY: I was at Hebrew school here—

MICHAEL: No bullshit, Joey.

JOEY: And the rabbi didn't want me.

MICHAEL: No bullshit.

JOEY: No bullshit. I was studying with the chazzan when my parents split up. I was a good student. If you can believe it. The chazzan used to say I was a good student.

My mother, her best friend was the rabbi's wife, Mrs. Kaplan. She was over for coffee all the time—especially after my father left. My best friends were the rabbi's kids. Moshe and Morry.

We didn't keep kosher—no traife in the house, no Hawaiian pizza, but just one set of dishes—but we kept kosher food and paper plates and plastic cups so they could visit.

Or we'd visit their place.

Or we'd play here.

MICHAEL: In the shul?

JOEY: I used to love it here—like your girl. I used to think G-d talked to me—not like Joan of Arc. I figured G-d talked to everyone. When you had good thoughts, that was G-d, and he was like the Big Sky Daddy. Bad thoughts, the devil. The devil talked to me a lot too. I still know the best place to sneak a cigarette here. If you ever want to have any more of this cancer medicine and not get caught.

Do you know where the dumb waiter is?

MICHAEL: There's a dumb waiter in here?

JOEY: By the furnace. There's a room behind it. Moshe and Morry and I . . . We used to play here. Then my mom stopped spending so much time with Mrs. Kaplan. I figured it was because she'd met my dad—he wasn't my dad yet.

MICHAEL: Your real father, your biological father—

JOEY: He left.

MICHAEL: And Mrs. Kaplan didn't approve of this new man.

JOEY: I'd never realized it until she met my dad—but I'd never seen my mom happy before.

Think about that for a minute. I'd never seen her happy.

What a crazy thing to realize as a kid. Twelve years old. And we'd talk about my bar mitzvah and what a big party we'd have. And my dad, he helped me write my speech, was so happy to help me write that speech. To honour my zayda.

(reciting/recalling) "Today I am a man, because today I am here to honour my family and my ancestors. Today I learn what it is to be a Jew and commit to honour my family, my forefathers and my people." My dad had never been to a bar mitzvah. He really wanted to go. And then I went for a class . . . and the rabbi was there—the rabbi was never at Hebrew school—and he yelled at me, told me I was stupid.

And when I reached out to touch the Torah . . . he hit my hand with his prayer book. Slammed it. Told me it wasn't for me. The Torah wasn't for me.

I didn't cry. I could barely move my hand for a week—it was purple for a week—but I didn't cry. And I didn't go back.

When I went to the car after and my mom saw my hand, that was my last class.

After that Moshe and Morry couldn't play with me anymore. The next week is Rosh Hashanah. Rabbi Kaplan is up on the bimah, talking about the new Holocaust, intermarriage, about how if you marry outside the faith you aren't a real Jew. If you marry outside the faith, your children aren't real Jews.

I was sitting with my zayda. He looked right at me when the rabbi said this. I decided if my mom wasn't a Jew anymore and I wasn't a Jew anymore I was leaving.

I got up. My zayda tried to stop me, but I got up and I walked out the back door of the shul. I know nobody's supposed to move when the rabbi is giving the sermon, nobody's supposed to go out the door.

So I walked out and I slammed the door.

That was the last time the rabbi talked to me, the last time the Big Sky Daddy talked to me.

The last time I went to shul.

When dad died, he couldn't be buried with the rest of our family, of course. So my mom—she wouldn't be buried in a Jewish cemetery either. Put it in her will. So Rabbi Kaplan was right. She stopped being Jewish.

And so did I.

MICHAEL: I'm sorry.

JOEY: You never hit me with a book. Not yet anyway. If you want to charge extra for the therapy session, feel free.

MICHAEL: Comes with the fancy office. If we kicked out everyone who married a non-Jew these days we'd have to turn out the lights.

JOEY: So non-Jews can participate here?

MICHAEL: It took a while. Every time we tried to open things up, Mr. Shapiro would go, "For this I survived the Holocaust," and everyone would shut up and we'd table things till the next meeting. Then his granddaughter Amber marries Charlie Wong and suddenly he's all about inclusion.

JOEY: We should study.

MICHAEL: What did G-d used to say?

JOEY: It was a long time ago.

MICHAEL: So that was it for you and G-d?

JOEY: I've got no problem with G-d. It's Jews I don't like.

And I sure as hell wasn't going to raise my daughter to be one. Last time I dated a Jewish girl I was ten. She punched me in the arm and that meant we were going steady.

So my mother, she gave up everything. When she was dying she . . . we wanted to call a rabbi. She wouldn't let us.

MICHAEL: I know that look. Just ask.

JOEY: It's nothing.

MICHAEL: Ask or you can buy your own joint.

JOEY: I was just wondering . . . what happens . . . what do you think happens . . . what do Jews believe happens . . .

MICHAEL: When we die.

JOEY: I told you, it's nothing, it's stupid, I'm sorry.

MICHAEL: It's what everyone wants to know.

According to my atheist friends, that's the only reason religions exist. Except for us and the Catholic church and the Masons. We exist to rule the world alongside our reptilian overlords.

So you want to know where we go when we die? Where Rachel's going?

JOEY: It's okay. Forget it.

MICHAEL: The Big Rock Candy Mountain. A cross between Disneyland and one of those fairy tale kingdoms run by a princess who found her prince and lived happily ever after.

JOEY: You believe that?

MICHAEL: She does . . . Of course she does. She grew up watching me do . . . this. Rachel wants to last long enough to be bat mitzvah. She doesn't want a ceremony, she just wants to be old enough to be called to the Torah. It would be easier if she wanted a pony or a trip to Disneyland, or a trip to Mars.

She's dying and she wants to be called to the Torah. I said, "We can do it early—we can do it now."

The bat mitzvah isn't even a real thing—not historically anyway. No one's gonna take my licence away if I call her to the Torah early. But Rachel, she grew up watching the rituals and she wants to do it properly. Like you.

"There are rules." That's what she told me. "There are rules. I have to be twelve." She's eleven, she believes in rules.

You think G-d believes in rules? Eleven-year-old girls. They believe in rules. They believe in happily ever after and they believe in rules. And

Rachel, she wants to be called to the Torah the day she turns twelve, so she can be a woman when she meets G-d.

JOEY: So what do you believe?

MICHAEL: Eleven-year-olds shouldn't die.

JOEY: You should start a religion. I'd join. I think even the atheists would be okay believing that.

MICHAEL: Are you okay to drive? I could use a lift. I ran here and . . . I could use a lift.

JOEY: Daniel—

MICHAEL: I could use a lift.

JOEY: We'll split a cab. My treat.

MICHAEL: A cab. A cab works.

JOEY: I have to tell you something.

MICHAEL: If it's about Daniel, not tonight, Joey.

JOEY: I don't really have glaucoma, but I had an aunt who had glaucoma so I could have glaucoma. I don't like lying to a rabbi.

MICHAEL: Do you want to try again?

He reaches for the joint.

The prayer. It's the one you lead to end the service.

JOEY: Sure.

MICHAEL starts—

MICHAEL: Adon olam.

JOEY: Adon olam.

TOGETHER: Asher malach, b'terem kol y'tzir nivra. L'et na'sah v'cheftzo kol, azai melech sh'mo nikra.

Adon olam.

MICHAEL exits As JOEY sings . . . the scene shifts as if he is now reading the contemporary version of Adon Olam at a service.

JOEY: V'acharey kichlot hakol, l'vado yimloch nora. V'hu haya, v'hu hoveh, v'hu yih'yeh b'tifara. V'hu echad, v'eyn sheni l'hamshil lo, l'hachbira.

B'li reishit, b'li tachlit, v'lo ha'oz v'hamisrah.

SCENE THIRTEEN

JOEY'S OFFICE

A few weeks later.

A direct echo of the opening scene. MICHAEL looks like the lawyer checking out JOEY's books.

Her back is to him.

JOEY: Excuse me.

MICHAEL: Sorry to disturb you.

JOEY: Rabbi?

MICHAEL: I never thought I'd have more books about sex than you do.

JOEY: I keep the good stuff at home. Plenty of sex in these books. But it's all in the penal codes. What did he do?

MICHAEL: I can't just come to visit?

JOEY: I'm so sorry. I know the look.

MICHAEL: My kid's dying of cancer. How am I supposed to look?

JOEY: That's a different look.

MICHAEL: How long have you been married?

JOEY: I've been married over thirty years. We're talking cumulatively, right?

MICHAEL: This is a mistake.

JOEY: This is my shul. I'm good at this.

MICHAEL: I've heard.

JOEY: If you'd rather pray . . .

MICHAEL: If I thought it would help.

JOEY: Maybe you should sit in my chair.

MICHAEL considers and takes him up on it.

Everyone tells me how it falls apart. When it fell apart. Half my billable hours people just want to talk. I used to tell them, a therapist is cheaper, a lot cheaper.

But they don't want therapy, they want revenge—they think they want revenge. And they think if I know their story, if I know all the ugly details, if I take their side, I'll get them their pound of flesh.

MICHAEL: And you do.

JOEY: I try . . .

I look for the lies they don't know about. The hidden bank accounts, the extra credit cards, investments.

It doesn't matter to me who fooled around with who, when or how many times someone forgot to do the dishes or missed an anniversary. And it doesn't matter to the courts either. But they usually think they want to know.

They may not even want revenge on their spouse—they want revenge on the fairy tale, on their parents, on whoever told them true love was forever and that once . . . someone like you said the magic words, they'd live happily ever after.

I don't need to know the story. But they tell me. And your story I hear all the time, and it's the only one that always breaks my heart.

This is where my job is like yours. I see people who've lost their faith in everything they ever believed in.

And thirty years of this I know your story—I know them all. They all start with, "You picked a fine time to leave me, Lucille." Book of Kenny Rogers.

MICHAEL: My story. You've been seeing other rabbis?

JOEY: The story that starts . . . everything was fine until our kid got sick.

MICHAEL *does not respond.*

I'm sorry. Usually I just listen. Except usually I get paid by the hour, so I like people to go on.

MICHAEL: We've only got forty minutes. Then I've got to see Rachel at the hospice. What do you usually ask first?

JOEY: Have you tried counselling?

MICHAEL: You want people to get counselling?

JOEY: As a lawyer I want them to hate each other. If they didn't hate each other when they decided to split, counselling will usually do it. For most people anyway—but you, maybe it'll help.

MICHAEL: Do you say that to all the girls?

JOEY: All my rabbis. It's okay, it's confidential here. Like when I talk to you. Like confession.

MICHAEL: Confession is a Catholic thing. I'm allowed to blab about whatever I want.

JOEY: I'm not. Legal thing. You can tell me anything.

MICHAEL mutters something.

I didn't—sorry—what did you say?

MICHAEL: It's too late for counselling. He's already left.

JOEY: One of the women at the hospice . . . Another parent? I'm so—

MICHAEL: No. I'd get that. I think I could live with that.

He left. I came home the other day and . . . this. Didn't call. Didn't text. Left a note.

She takes out the note.

How . . . Russian.

JOEY reads it. He can't believe what he's reading.

JOEY: Jesus Christ.

MICHAEL: Yah. That's what I said.

JOEY: Jesus Christ.

MICHAEL: I never . . . I just never . . .

JOEY: I'm so sorry. That son of a bitch.

MICHAEL: Some people aren't good with pain.

JOEY: There's no excuse.

MICHAEL: No. No excuses. But maybe no surprises either. When my mother met Daniel, she told me she loved him—told me he was a beautiful man with a beautiful heart, told me he'd been born blessed—good looks, brains, a loving family, money—told me I shouldn't marry him.

JOEY wants to ask, but waits instead . . .

I thought . . . I didn't talk to her for a week . . . thought she was telling me she didn't think I was good enough for him.

She said that wasn't it at all, that he'd lived such a beautiful life, that he'd never been scarred, never been tested.

Most of us had pain early.

Survived . . . something.

Survived too much.

Our battle scars heal—but we've got them—and our scars make us stronger.

Everything came so easy to Daniel.

She said as long as everything went well, he'd be perfect for me. But this is life, and that means things don't always go well, and one day something would go wrong and maybe he'd be okay, maybe he'd rise to the occasion, but probably, because he'd never had to fight for anything ever, he'd shatter like glass.

Rachel . . . if she makes it through this . . . she'll be as strong as Wonder Woman.

JOEY: I didn't think . . . she might be okay?

MICHAEL's pain answers this: no.

She stares at the note, reads it in a Russian accent.

MICHAEL: Dear Mikala, I've gone home. I can't watch Rachel go through this anymore. I'm so sorry, but I'm not as brave as you are. I need to live my own life. I will always love you both.

JOEY: What does he mean, home? I thought he was from Russia. Where did he go?

MICHAEL: Russia.

JOEY: He . . . what?

MICHAEL: Fucking coward. Fucking coward. Who does this? Who does this to their kid?

JOEY: You want to break something?

MICHAEL: I called his cell. As soon as I saw the note, I called. His mother answered the phone. His mother. She said he'd call me—when he was ready. I couldn't ask when he'd be ready because Anna doesn't speak English. So he told her what to say, told her and made her memorize it.

Made his mother memorize it.

"Daniel vill call ven he is ready."

What am I supposed to tell Rachel?

JOEY: How much you love her.

MICHAEL: What do you tell people who want revenge?

JOEY: That they'll have to settle for money. Or—

He stops himself.

MICHAEL: Custody.

That's the other one, right. There's no money to fight over. And he's not fighting for custody.

JOEY: Maybe he'll come back.

MICHAEL: I hope so . . . Then I can kill him . . . Isn't this where you say something clever?

JOEY: Sorry.

MICHAEL: What do I tell Rachel? What am I supposed to tell Rachel?

JOEY: That her dad loves her and then . . . are rabbis allowed to lie? Because if I were you, I'd lie. He's building a new house for you. He's buying her a pony. He's catching her a pony. He's curing cancer. He's on a secret mission in outer space to cure cancer. Anything. Just tell her he loves her . . . That he'll come back for her bat mitzvah.

MICHAEL: I can't do this anymore.

JOEY: Can't . . .

MICHAEL: Believe. Tell people to believe.

JOEY: You're a great rabbi.

MICHAEL: You want to order pizza? Hawaiian? On me.

They sit together a moment and then . . .

I've got to . . . I need to get Rachel.

MICHAEL *exits.* JOEY *sits alone, processing.*

JOEY: Shit.

SCENE FOURTEEN

THE BIMAH

Three weeks later.

MICHAEL *enters. She is holding a prayer book with a cute pink book cover on it (think* My Little Pony, *unicorns or kitties). She looks up at the eternal light.*

MICHAEL *silently mouths the words to a prayer. "Shma yisrael, adonai eloheinu adonai echad."*

She holds the prayer book. She considers the eternal light.

MICHAEL: Three days. You couldn't have waited three fucking days?

And she tosses the prayer book at the light and shatters it, leaving us in black. She does not move for a long time.

SCENE FIFTEEN

RABBI'S OFFICE

Thursday night.

JOEY *waits.*

And waits.

The intercom crackles.

SHERYL: Mr. Brant, I told you, she hasn't come in since . . .

SHERYL starts to cry.

JOEY: I'll wait. We have a class.

He looks at the books and he waits . . .

SCENE SIXTEEN

JOGGING PATH

A week or two later.

MICHAEL is running. She is in her running gear. Her head is not covered. And she approaches . . . JOEY at a bench, waiting.

JOEY: Hey.

MICHAEL keeps running. Oblivious to him.

HEY!

MICHAEL stops. Startled.

MICHAEL: Joey?

JOEY: I'm so sorry.

MICHAEL: It was good to see you at shiva. Thank you.

JOEY: How are you doing?

When are you coming back to shul?

I can't do my bar mitzvah without you.

MICHAEL: You don't need me.

JOEY: Cantor Putin is running the services.

MICHAEL: I'm taking time off.

JOEY: You should be in shul.

MICHAEL: For what?

JOEY: For you, for G-d, for—

MICHAEL: I don't have anything to say to G-d right now.

JOEY: I'm sure you do. Just not what's in the books about how great He is.

MICHAEL: So I have nothing to say to G-d in public. I'm sorry, Joey. I can't.

JOEY: You got me there.

MICHAEL: And you got me here.

JOEY: No. Daniel doesn't get to win. He doesn't get custody of your faith. It's worth more than the house.

MICHAEL: Not in this market.

JOEY: Michael.

MICHAEL: This isn't about Daniel. It's not about Rachel. It's about me. I can't be there for anybody else—how do I counsel people when . . . no.

JOEY: You tell them you understand their pain and they know you're telling the truth.

MICHAEL: Faith and me . . . Irreconcilable differences.

JOEY: So you're telling me Rachel believed she was going to a better place and you don't?

MICHAEL looks ready to kick him. Instead she starts to run away.

Is running away literal, or a metaphor?

MICHAEL: Sometimes things are both.

And MICHAEL runs away as JOEY watches her go.

SCENE SEVENTEEN

JOEY'S OFFICE

A few days later.

Night. JOEY is singing his Torah portion, alone.

JOEY: Vayiqrah eilav mala. Adonai min hashamayim, vayomer, "Avraham, Avraham!" Vayomer—

MICHAEL: Hineni.

She steps into the light. Dressed in civvies. Her head is not covered.

Here I am. And he said, "Do not stretch forth your hand to the lad, nor do the slightest thing to him, for now I know that you are a G-d-fearing man, and you did not withhold your son, your only one, from Me."

JOEY: G-d can be a shit.

MICHAEL: So I've heard. You're sounding good.

JOEY: I've been skipping poker nights.

MICHAEL: Nervous?

JOEY: Curious.

MICHAEL: You're not finding religion on me, are you, Yosef?

JOEY laughs.

JOEY: I don't believe the Big Sky Daddy is deciding who wins baseball games or even who wins wars. There are too many shitty things that happen for me to believe someone's keeping track of everyone everywhere—except Santa Claus. But I saw everyone at the shiva for Rachel, I saw Benny and Sandee and I thought . . . there's something . . . something in this.

MICHAEL: You want some help practising for next week?

JOEY: You offering?

MICHAEL: I . . . have to . . . I cashed your cheque. I'll pay you back.

JOEY: It's okay, you earned it. You taught me a lot.

MICHAEL: Not enough to cover tuition to Harvard. That was a big cheque.

JOEY: I'm a challenging student.

MICHAEL: It's just . . . I'm not working right now and Daniel . . . He's trying to take the house. He's trying to take everything. Why would he do that?

JOEY: He has to blame somebody. It's what we do.

MICHAEL: He's trying to evict me.

JOEY: It won't happen.

MICHAEL: I can't do this.

JOEY: You won't. This is the part of the job where I get to do a mitzvah or two.

MICHAEL: I can't afford you.

JOEY: Come to shul next week. We'll call it even.

MICHAEL: I can't.

JOEY: Because you don't believe in the Sky Daddy either?

MICHAEL: I just . . . I don't know what I believe right now.

JOEY: If you don't tell anyone, I won't.

MICHAEL: It's not right.

JOEY: I'm not doing it without you.

MICHAEL: You have to. For Benny. You've done so much work. You skipped poker nights.

JOEY: No, I don't need it anymore. I decided if I could tell you what I told you . . . I could tell my daughter. I told her after the last night of shiva for Rachel.

MICHAEL: (*delighted*) She understood.

JOEY: No, I don't think so. It doesn't fit the way she sees the world.

MICHAEL: Too many shades of grey.

JOEY: Some people aren't good with pain.

MICHAEL: No.

JOEY: She didn't understand my reasons, but I think she understood I had reasons. That was news to her. I invited her, invited Benny.

Benny thought it was hilarious.

I invited everyone.

MICHAEL: You don't need me there.

JOEY: Yeah, I do.

MICHAEL exits. JOEY puts on his tallis.

SCENE EIGHTEEN
BIMAH

Bar mitzvah day.

The eternal light is repaired and on. JOEY *is in tallis.*

JOEY: Thank you all for coming.

My Torah portion is about Abraham, about faith—about something I've always thought was ridiculous. Seriously, Abraham offers to kill his son for G-d?

But then the rabbi taught me how to see his sacrifice as a metaphor. What could be more profound for anyone than . . . losing a child. And what could be more powerful than losing a child and carrying on . . . for your community . . . for your world . . . For your child.

When I started this journey, when I returned to this shul for the first time since I was my grandson's age, it was all for Benny. I thought it was all for Benny. And for Tzeporah.

I never imagined it would be for me. Or for Rabbi Levitz-Sharon. Or for Rachel.

I think of the bar mitzvah I almost had here and the speech I wrote with my dad. The speech I never gave.

I still remember a bit of it:

"Today I am a man, because today I am here to honour my family and my ancestors. Today I learn what it is to be a Jew and commit to honour my family, my forefathers and my people."

So it's not Shakespeare—I was twelve.

Rachel wanted this more than anything—to stand here—to celebrate being a Jew, being with all of you, being one of us—because that's what the ceremony is about. It's not about becoming an adult, it's about becoming a member of a community with rights and responsibilities. When I started I believed . . . that I was better off without this place. But spending time here, I'm reminded of the power of community. And sometimes faith is all we have and all we need. Okay, faith . . . and a good lawyer.

Today . . . today as I look out at my friends, my daughter, my grandson, I am a member of this community, our community led by this rabbi. Today I am a man.

MICHAEL: Today you are a man.

And I welcome you to this community. I hope you'll all join us for a reception afterwards.

JOEY: Kosher wine really isn't as bad as it used to be.

MICHAEL: And remember, renovations on the auditorium start next week. It's the season for renewal. For hope.

For faith that this year—this year—things will be better.

Now please join our bar mitzvah boy in Adon Olam—

JOEY: Adon olam.

MICHAEL: Adon olam.

JOEY: Asher malach.

MICHAEL: Asher malach.

JOEY: B'terem kol.

MICHAEL: B'terem kol.

JOEY: Y'tzir nivra. L'et na'asah.

MICHAEL: L'et na'asah.

BOTH: V'cheftzo kol.
V'cheftzo kol, azai melech. Sh'mo nikra.
Adon olam . . .

They finish in harmony and—

Blackout—except for the eternal flame.

GLOSSARY

Consider including this in the program. Audience members suggested this in talkbacks at the premiere production.

Alav ha shalom: Peace be upon him.

Aliyah: Being called to the Torah *or* when someone Jewish makes a pilgrimage to Israel and stays.

Bar mitzvah: Watch/read the play . . .

Bimah: The altar.

Chazzan: A synagogue official—in this case, the synagogue official who taught bar mitzvah boys.

Kippah: Head covering (a sign of respect for G-d).

Kosher: Food (or combinations of food) that are acceptable to eat according to Jewish law.

Lubavitcher: A member of an orthodox sect of Judaism.

Minyan: The ten adults required to hold a prayer service. In orthodox services those adults (over thirteen) must be male.

Ner tamid: The eternal light—found in every synagogue.

Shiva: Mourning services.

Tefillin: Two boxes that contain portions of the Torah that are wrapped around the head and heart for certain prayer services.

Tikkun olam: Repair of the world. Think kosher karma.

Traife: Not kosher (e.g., Hawaiian pizza).

Yahrzeit: Mourning prayer.

Yeshiva: Where rabbis learn how to become rabbis.

Zayda: Grandfather.

Zikhrono livrakha: "May his memory be a blessing."

THANK YOUS

Thanks and todah to my official and unofficial spiritual advisors: Rabbi Harry Brechner, Judy and Art Dodek, Sandee Huberman, Rabbi Laura Duhan Kaplan, Art Norris, Rabbi Wilfred Solomon, Heather Wolfe, Rabbi Yosef Wosk and Ben Wosk. Thanks to the people who sparked some of the ideas that inspired this story—especially Stephen Kaplan, Michael Petrasek and Emma Young.

Bar Mitzvah Boy was originally workshopped by my UBC Playwriting Masterclass with Stephen Hunt. Thanks to everyone in the class—especially Polly Pokheev and Georgina Beatty. I was in that workshop because Rayne Benu pretty much told me I was getting my master's degree.

My amazing original private reading/workshop team was Rayne, Graham Croft, Ian Ferguson, Howie Siegel and Kirsten Van Ritzen.

Thanks to David Winitsky, Annie Meisels, Philip Hoffman and everyone else involved with the Jewish Playwriting Contest for all your advice and support.

Thanks to everyone at Pacific Theatre and Chester Theatre for bringing this story to life.

And thanks to everyone at Playwrights Canada Press for this beautiful book.

Mark Leiren-Young has written over two dozen plays, including dramas, comedies, musicals, revues and theatre for young audiences. His play *Shylock* has been produced around the world since debuting at Bard on the Beach in Vancouver in 1996. The Czech production of the play ran for three years in Prague and was broadcast as a television special in 2019. He won the 2009 Leacock Medal for Humour for his bestselling memoir *Never Shoot a Stampede Queen*. He lives in Victoria, BC. You can find out more about Mark at leiren-young.com.

First edition: April 2020
Printed and bound in Canada by Rapido Books, Montreal

Jacket design by Rayne E. Benu
Jacket photo © iStock.com/TinaFields
Author photo © Mark Halliday

PLAYWRIGHTS CANADA PRESS

202-269 Richmond St. W.
Toronto, ON
M5V 1X1

416.703.0013
info@playwrightscanada.com
www.playwrightscanada.com
@playcanpress